Restoring
The
Queen

Restoring The Queen

Laini Mataka

DuForcelf

Restoring The Queen

A DuForcelf book published by Black Classic Press 1994
All rights reserved
Library of Congress Catalog Card No. 91-74131
ISBN 0-933121-80-6
Cover art by Julee Dickerson Thompson
Backcover photo by Ronnie Wooten

Printed by BCP Digital Printing, *a division of Black Classic Press*

Founded in 1978, Black Classic Press specializes in bringing to light obscure and significant works by and about people of African descent. If our books are not available in your area, ask your local bookseller to order them. Our current list of titles can be obtained by writing:

Black Classic Press
c/o List
P.O. Box 13414
Baltimore, MD 21203

A Young Press With Some Very Old Ideas

To The Queens Who Hold Court In My Heart

Harriet Tubman, Sis. Nzinga, Ida B. Wells, Januwa, Nannie Burroughs, Loogie, Fannie Lou Hamer, Eisha, Yaa Assantewa, Isisara, Queen Nzinga, Rose Ann, Dr. Frances Welsing, Jackie, L. Cress-Love, Sadiqua, Hon. Maxine Waters, Talibah, Dr. Rosalind Jeffries, Majiza, Ntozake Shange, Renee, Jayne Cortez, Ainah, June Jordan, Veroneca, Inez McCullough, Tashi, Edna Parker, Olufunmilayo, Ann Pettiford, Tama, Jan Campell, Vanessa, Assata Shakur, Julie D., Cheryl, Freeda-*my honey-brown sistah*

And to the Greatest of them all:
Mildred Robinson

To The Kings Under Whose Rule I Flourish

Chancellor Williams, Cheikh Anta Diop, John G. Jackson, Imani Lumumba, Gabriel Prosser, Denmark Vesey, Nat Turner, Jonathan Jackson, George Jackson, Mark Essex, John Harvey, Ronnie Wooten, Sun-Ra, Dr. Yosef ben-Jochannan, Dr. John H. Clarke, Emmanuel Ndiaye, Dr. John Chissell, Mohamed Turay, Dr. B. Marshall, Ahmad Onyango, Dr. Asa Hilliard, Mike, Doc, Acklyn Lynch, Junie, Kalamu Ya Salaam, Ako, Haki Madhubuti, Mamadi, Pharoah Sanders, Duck, Dugger, Gil-Scott Heron, Paul Coates, Uziki, Ta-nehisi

Thanks also to:

Sweet Honey in the Rock, The Yawa Family, 2000 Black Family, Ta-Nefer Ankh, Union Temple, Ujamaa Shule, WPFW, Kankouran, African Heritage Dancers and Drummers, My good neighbors on Belmont St.

Table of Contents

the void-fillers

creatures with an incredible sense of timing
can sniff loneliness out in a crowd
can change the body's form into any size
that will insure entry into any crack or crevice
yr heart accidentally leaves un-sealed.

they always know just what to say to cause u
to suspend logic long enuff
for them to attain significance in yr life.

& yes, there are moments that over-flow with
honey. u may even get to sing
a minor rhapsody or two
but in the end u wind up
with more blues than lightnin hopkins,
bessie smith & muddy waters.

cuz u've been hit — by a void-filler.

somebody who always wants to come to yr house
to be entertained. always eatin yr food,
drinkin yr drinks, & receiving the blessings
from yr body. dont never bring nothin but
their tired selves. never wants
to go where money must be spent.
always ready to groove on yr friendships
while never introducing u into any.

until one day u just wake up, drained.
u turn over in bed, and there's the drainer
wantin to kno what's for break-fast.

when u start to shower/the realizations fall
like rain. how the hell did u let this happen?
& for a moment u almost hate yrself
for having been human enuff to experience
the kind of hunger that paves the way
for a void-filler:

a creature u wld never have chosen
during times of abundance. somebody
u probably wldnt even have looked at,
under normal circumstances.
a being who specializes in discovering people
who're at an all-time low.

& as long as u have something to give/they
will stick with u. and the only way to get
rid of one is by asking for a commitment.
only be careful to cover yr face, so the
dust wont get in yr eyes as the void-filler
hauls ass/good-bye to rescue someone else
from the abomitable feeling of being un-luv'd
& alone.

amandla

(for Chris Hani & Oliver Tambo)

bones are dancing blood inflaming
blistering town-ships into purging actions.

chalk-faced pillagers are scared shitless
of the total, righteousness will finally exact.
though armed to the max/they think they can
elude karma by hiding in their ostentatious
fortresses, while their consciences stand at
attention in anticipation of the ultimate
confrontation with Blacks/driven almost insane
by their obsession to remain on their own land.

& the bones are dancing blood
thru the shattered glass of splintered nites.
where the dead come back to life & terror takes
a more accurate form/becomes a living thing
this time stalking witeness.

meanwhile,
pale-faced pillagers pray to their god for safety
but their god/being only the president of an
illegal regime/ can only do so much.

he cannot stop the bones from dancing.
& he cannot stop the blood from flowing thru
the torture-chambered detention centers
where the bones are in a frenzy & spreading
the bones are breakdancing and spreading
the dead have been raised/they are dancing
with the living, and neither
are afraid . . .

noriega

u shlda died first.
before u allowed yr country
to be given up to the enemy
u shlda died first.
even yr blood-stained monies
cldve bought u a place to stay.
if u had read the cards right
steada layin up
on the good ship lollipop
u wldve known
it was time to get away.
and when gettin away
started gettin out of yr hands,
u shlda died.
leavin a list of amerikan high-top names
that wldve brought bush-ism to its syphilitic knees.
u shlda died.
before u let them take, take, take, u
to a where from which u will never return.
u shlda died,
before u chumped out on yr country
by turning yr manly face
into a pine-apple disgrace.
before u let amerika use the destiny of yr people
for toilet tissue,
either, u shlda died,
or some real panamanian nationalist
shlda killed u.

the barbarians are stretching out

(for Somalia)

for eons,
it has become a heavily relied upon tradition for wite
people to dump on us.
they dumped us around the world
so that we cld take care of them no matter where. then,
they went back to our homes
and dumped christianity on our loved ones
encouraging them to relinquish the memory
of the names of our gods
and surrender their identities to the melting pot.
then, they dumped their educational shit on us
so that no matter how we'd look at our problems
we wld never betray wite interests to solve them.
then, they dumped their deadly ways on us,
knowing that once we adopted them,
we wld annihilate ourselves.
then, they dumped foul information on us
when we foolishly enlisted their expertise
in the prevention of desertifcation
and deforestation.
then, they dumped AIDS on us
to get our natural resources
and to see how the rest of the world wld respond.
and now, their hatred for us
has reached a new zenith.
they are dumping toxic waste into afrika .
so that all things of color
must die or mirror witeness.
they are dumping chemical waste into afrika,
so that they can complete the circle of atrocities
which their ancestors began.
they are dumping their technologically superior waste
into afrika so that the people can die

amerikan deaths
even tho they refused to live amerikan-like.

are we gonna always be dumpsters for wite people? are
we gonna always be receptacles for wite-isms?

are they gonna always be able
to substitute our brains for toilet bowls?

& if not, then when is this pattern going to stop?
anybody gotta watch?

hope

hope that one day,
u will stop whining & crying about yr childhood
& grow up before senility sets in.

hope that one day,
u will stop talkin bout how much
u luv & respect Black women
& pull up your pants.

hope that one day, u will realize
that u are not the only person on the planet
with awesome talents.

hope that one day, you will learn to treat people
the way u want them to treat u.

hope that one day, yr spiritual self
will blossom into something greater
than a seedling in the dark.

hope that one day, u will learn
to develop yr inner-self with the same passion
u use on yr physical self.

hope that one day, u will learn
to luv unconditionally
& not throw people away
when they dont turn out the way
u want them to.

hope that one day, u will learn
to understand women instead of writing their
emotions off as hysteria.

hope that one day, u will learn
to listen to criticism
like u luv to hear praise.

hope that one day, u will learn
to be as humble as u often pretend to be.

hope that one day, u will learn
to maintain the same set of values
during bad times, that u do in good times.

hope that one day, u will learn
that macho aint mucho
& being emotionally retarded
aint nothin to brag about.

hope that one day, u will discover
that all yr life
u've been living with a safety net under u
& that the net-holders
are tired of yr charming smile.

hope that one day, u will stop
expecting people to do for u
what u can & shld do for yrself.

hope that one day, u will learn
to appreciate yr friends for reasons greater than
what they can do for u.

hope that one day, u will learn
to live within yr means,
especially when u havent any.

hope that one day, u will wake up
& smell the coffee, tea & orange juice.

hope that one day, u will discover
that God did not create the universe
for yr convenience.

hope that until u stop acting like a child
u never have one.

I hope u kno that this pome is about u
but given its accuracy,
i doubt it.

to the sweet young thang in 106

if i was really a huzzy
u wld be toppin the icing on my cake
right about now.
if i was really what some people think i am
i wld be gleaming the tip of yr. . .
& not caring, at all, whether u remembered me next week
or not. if
i was really that wild, u'd be tongue-lashin me
into acquiescence &
i'd be screamin yr name into the ethers
while the neighbors placed bets on
whether or not we were doin it.

if these were the sensuous '70s
we'd be freakin out on the possibilities
doing pretzel dances on the ceilings
& writin testimonials on bein satisfied
in non-algebraic terms.

but these are the nasty '90s
& until i get psychic enuff to kno
on those infrequent times when i play russian
roulette/which chamber the bullet is really in
u'll have to blaze new hedonistic trails w/out me.

now that the price of saying yes has been lowered

(for parents and teens considering the use of Norplant)

she can say yes to him
who has been worrying her to death
about access to her dark & moist.
now she can say yes to him
whose entire existence was almost jeopardized
by the thought that she might say no
now she can say yes to him
who hates condoms, cuz a real man
does it in the raw.
& now she can really say yes to him
who thinx hygiene is
wipin his face in the morning.
now she can say yes to him
whose drippings go un-checked
from coochie to coochie.
& now she can say yes to him
& all his companions:
trichomoniasis, gonorrhea, chlamydia, syphilis, herpes
& the big "A".

now that she can say yes,
he can fun & run & preserve
that aspect of slavery
that turned Blackmen out as studs.
a penis from which a body grew
& developed everything except
a sense of man-hood.
now, that she can give it up
& he can get it w/out havin to worry
about makin a baby
they can screw themselves

into an infectious wonderland. anything.
just dont make a baby.
cuz we adults are tired inside & out
& we dont feel like baby-sitting.

still believers

(for Kurt Schmoke)

we kno they gave the Native Amerikans smallpox
infected blankets, as a sophisticated form of birth control
      & still we believe.

we kno they gave syphilis to Black inmates in tuskegee
just to see how ravishing it cld be
      & still we believe.

we kno they secretly sterilized huge portions of the
Native Amerikan population
      & still we believe.

we kno they murdered over 900 Black people
in Jonestown/who they claimed killed themselves
      & still we believe.

we kno they dropped agent orange on their own
servicemen in vietnam
      & still we believe.

we kno they'll knife breasts that aren't lethal &
carve out wombs that aren't malignant
      & still we believe.

we kno they'll cut a baby out of a woman when
they're tired of waitin for the baby to come by itself
      & still we believe.

we kno they import or create all the drugs that
Black people will ever embrace
      & still we believe.

we kno they feed ritalin into the blood-streams
of young Black males to curb their tendencies towards
kingliness
      & still we believe.

we kno they killed nat turner, jonathan & george,
malcolm, king, the hostages at attica, bessie & cabral
        & still we believe.

that we can trust them to put 5 capsules full of dope into
our bodies that will not hurt us, but suspend motherhood,
w/out internal damage. we trust them so much we're
even willing to submit our children to them & their faintly
nazi-like experiments.

& even tho we kno that their survival on this planet is
determined by their domination of people who look like
us we still believe
       & hand them the flowers
           of our young womanhood,
               on a silver platter.

make u wanna holler & throw up...

(for the druggie-boys)

the living dead are far more dangerous
than the already dead,
becuz they dont kno they're dead
becuz they're fixed on the life in u
which they feed on like hip-hop maggots
tryin to enliven their willfully dead selves.
they've got dying down to a fine science
of not hearing
       not seeing
           not saying
              anything that is life-affirming.

everyday is just like the day before
and all tomorrows are arrived at unexpectedly
& ungraciously,
while next week is a myth
& next year is a conceptual impossibility.

and though u rise each morning
pushing yr way up thru the funk & despair
with arms that reach out to God & sun,
yr momentum glows with potential
til u step outside
& yr energy is stalked & sapped
by the living-dead
who dont kno they're dead
even though their epithets are carved
into the solid rock of the crack they sell
while they slither around in the day-time
waiting for the darkness of night
to cover them as they celebrate
the monotony of their own impotence.

the heroes of wine wall

at first sight
our hero looks deformed.
he was not born with a hump on his back
but he carries one just the same.
as a reminder
of his waning brilliance, & dead companions.
Black joe, sweet willie, & big ben
the womanizin, terrorizin trio
who once cheered his ability to hold
his liquor & raise the skirts of
women who swore never.

    they're all dead now.

safely tucked away in amerika's closet
their skeletons rattle in un-ceasing rebellion.
but we dont listen
cuz we too busy talkin bout how hip they usta be before
they took to
altering the world thru their senses.
we preach instead of teach
& our messages end up as snot-rags
in the back pockets of heroes
whose victories were never acknowledged
or rewarded beyond their personal
honorary positions

    on wine wall.

please urge my blossoming

u'd be so easy to curl up to.
the darkness of u is so solid that it forms a security that makes me
want to yield and blossom into
the night flower of yr most succulent imaginings.
u'd be so easy to cherish—so easy to revere.
i can see me now, seeking refuge in yr arms and asylum
in yr eyes.
everything in me just opens up to u
reaching beyond the levels marked *danger*
that i set for myself.
u'd be so easy to cater to,
so easy to be thankful for, so easy to be afraid of, so easy
to curse in loving intonations.
yr consistency challenges the very foundation
of my memory—which is rooted
in wrong time, wrong man, wrong evaluations—
and yet,

though my fear sends u away
my heart begs u to stay

      and be the one to urge my blossoming.

consummation

(for Darnell)

Nangwaya screams in the night!
thinx he's a wolf baying at the moon.
and everytime he cries,
his voice is a jet plane
and my soul is the sound barrier,
breaking.

karma can find you
even when social services cant

caught like naked jelly
in the chill of the same old blues
the people of the earth are tired of u
and if u were to split right now,
no one wld even miss u or plead yr case.
cuz u chose against life, to be a
genocidal hitman.
u chose in the face of all that was
afrikan and good, to use yr body against nature.
to sow yr own seeds without ever
coming back to harvest.
and now u are caught and suspended,
far away from all human feelings.
u sit all bent over
a warped manifestation of yr own deeds.
a stranger to yr own children
and too weak, to even dance

a warrior's death.

murder

tell me my sistah,
have u committed murder lately
have u swallowed poison, lost yr mind
and kept a child from its father lately.

have u put yrself first
by bad-mouthing someone
whose touch u ustah die for.
have u become hard, and bitter and ugly
becuz u felt compelled to murder the memory
of a man whose luv u cldnt keep?

have u murdered yr son, lately
have u taken his future as a man
and tied it to the railroad tracks
becuz his father failed to luv u back, forever?

have u robbed yr daughter
of a positive relationship
with the first man she ever knew.
have u killed her desire to luv a man
by recounting war stories
that still have u shell-shocked beyond belief.
have u murdered anyone lately?

have u drawn and court'd anyone, lately
not becuz they cldnt pay child-support
but becuz they left u for higher heights.
not becuz they now whisper promises in a new ear
but becuz *no one* whispers *anything* in yr ear.
have u kept a child
away from its father lately?

not becuz the father was a junkie,
a rapist,
a child-molester.
a basher,

a walking-talking horror;
but, becuz u want to hurt him.
becuz u cant find any place to dispose of yr pain.
have u put yr child's life
and future development in jeopardy
becuz u cant get pass yr own pain.
must i ask again?

have u committed murder lately?
have u kept a Blackman away from his child?

consumer addicts

can anybody deny the fact
that niggahs luv to buy?
luv to let u kno how much they spent for this or that
even when it's plain to see it wasnt worth it.

niggahs shop around for clothes
made by wite designers
who stole their ideas from non-wite designers.
they luv to wear the names of wite people
on their behinds,
like their ancestors wore the brands
of their masters on their thighs.

niggahs have gone kente and mud-cloth crazy
w/out the slightest notion as to
where they came from or once signified.
even chicken-hearted colonel sanders
is making his employees wear kente-like uniforms
to bring in the dollars from the afrikan community.

niggahs wear the liberation colors
becuz they think it's chic
yet they dont kno the meaning of the colors,
and wldnt miss a t.v. show to find out.
some niggahs even wear leather confederate caps
as if they longed for slavery, dixie and mammy too.

with afrika bein the in-thing,
niggahs wear clothes from "the continent"
w/out knowin or carin about their significance.
women wear kufis meant for men,
and pants meant for boys.
but it's alright, becuz this is amerika
where nothin means anything anyway.
so the afrikan custom
of piercing the ears in several places,
or piercing the nose

is copied w/out regard to custom,
or tribe or country.
women who can't remember their names
wear great big hussy earrings
with all three names inside,
to go along with their wing-tip hairdos
which cost as much as $80 a throw,
and come in every color imaginable/
except those colors natural to human hair.
did i say hair?
for the right price, any kinda hair
can be woven onto any kinda head
and made to look ludicrously, natural.

niggahs buy 3 feet worth of pants
to fit 2 feet worth of legs.
they buy caps with brims and wear them backwards
to show which direction they're goin in,
as they race towards the 21st century
with their clothes turned inside out.

niggahs will buy anything
with Malcolm X on it as they sell drugs,
beat up their women, and deny their children.
then they buy pacifiers to suck on
til some young woman offers her titties.

niggahs buy high heels
to keep them high, in the air
and away from the ground
where everything for niggahs
is very real and very deadly.

brown legs spike themselves up on heels
which do not allow them to run in a country
that specializes in makin niggahs run for their lives.

niggahs buy gold
as if they were really goin somewhere.
perhaps this is reminiscent of ancient grandeur,
but all too often the gold is bought at the expense

of otha more significant things,
    like their children's education.

niggahs lead the world
in the purchasing of sweatsuits
and elaborate tennis shoes
that never see a day's worth of exercise.
reeboks. adidas. and nikes.
can dip into their pockets anytime they want to,
but when it comes to buying a computer for their
children, they cant afford it.

but they can afford to buy perms
to permanently destroy the only kind of hair
their heads will ever grow.
relaxers for the kiddies, a curl-free for mommy,
and a jheri for daddy.
and johnson's manufacturers go to the bank
while the the Black family goes on welfare
to raise funds for a ticket to the nut-house.

niggahs will buy anything u tell them to buy.
obscene t-shirts, spandex, tight yeast-infectious jeans,
tinted contact lenses,
afrikan prints made in holland,
kente-looking strips made by koreans
and on and on and on.

niggahs buy books written by liars
who claim afrikans have contributed nothin
to civilization, when in fact, afrikans are civilization.

niggahs buy artwork
that doesnt reflect anything that is them.
they buy symbols like crucifixes
to ward off the very evil they have *come* to represent.

niggahs buy vcrs and compact discs
and a host of electrical devices
that never seem to work
when it's time to build a nation.

niggahs buy sat. nite specials
that they use especially on sat. nites
but only on otha niggahs
and nevah on their real enemies.
and everybody oughta kno by now,
that the only reason niggahs are still alive,
is so they can make the things
they'll eventually have to buy.
and niggahs will *buy. buy. buy.*

cable t.v. w/out ever considering
the possibility that cable might receive
as well as transmit.
u walk into some homes,
and the screen is the first thing that hits u/like a great
big eye.

and niggahs will buy sunglasses
to keep out the light of knowing
who they truly are, *the original lightmakers.*

niggahs buy essence magazine,
and then they buy whatever essence tells them to buy
so they can find true luv holdin up the wall
at some disco/along with a million
otha sistahs all waitin for one
of the 10.5 heterosexual bros to ask them
to dance or romance or run away to the
islands where they can constitute
beautiful absurdity forever.

niggahs buy eye-make-up
so that when they look into the mirror
their eyes can continuously deny
what the mirror will always imply:
we are an afrikan people,
not amerikan... whatever that is,
it certainly makes niggahs wanna buy
more suburban houses to hide in,
better clothes to look ignorant in,

and finer coffins to be buried in by crackas,
who thru technotrikology
will help niggahs to stop buyin,
and start dyin *for real*

the desert storm patriot

and when u say amerika
his balls tingle
& his testosterone sizzles
true. to the red, white and blu
he will jam anywhere he can
for God and cuntry.

and when he dies,
the govt will give him a 21 gun salute.
one shot for every snatch he managed to stretch.

and when they lower him into the ground
his ex-lovers will whisper
about what a bum lay he was
while the women he raped,
wait
to dig him up and kill him again.

stun-gunned by the dumb

(for Sayeed)

he sd he was an afrikan.
that i
didnt understand
that he was from anotha culture,
where
it was alright to hit a woman
                hit a woman
                hit a woman!

as long as she was not made to bleed.
it was alright
to correct her when she did something wrong.
and i sd
a woman is not someone
u slap around
to discipline like a child
or a dog.
and he sd he'd never hit an animal
becuz they cant talk.

??

i hung up the phone!
becuz i luv afrikans and
i cant stand male-impersonators
with accents or attitudes.

pullin the coat of the un-incarcerated

(for Marshall Eddie Conway and Terrance Johnson)

whether u can dig it or not
we are all inmates of the same society.

we cannot go anywhere,
anytime we want to.
we cannot take care of
and be responsible for
our own becuz
we have no scientific means
of supporting ourselves.

we depend upon the same people
(who are endangering our species)
for the mini-jobs we slave at
just so's we can eat & sleep in a bldg.
& have a change of european rags.

our prison:

is so big, so vast,
so spacious
u cant even see the bars
(as they sprout up in the minds of our young)
that's why most of us
dont believe we doin time.
so we act like we're outside
til the trap door opens
and we feel ourselves falling, falling, falling
into a hell that has no end.

prisons:

werent just made for criminals
but also for people who are caught

thinking, or havin a dream
that was not designed by wite people.
(and right now somebody probably wants to remind me
that wite people go to jail too; but this pome aint about
them)

so when they catch u here
actin like u might kno who they are
and what they're doin
they come at'chu a thousand strong
kick down any and all doors,
and drag u outa the house
so's yr family can instantly die of shame
a million times,
for being too powerless to stop them!

and a lotta times, it looks like the end
only they dont always wanna kill u
they just wanna put'chu under the microscope
to see why u aint crazi
    and
       or dead. cuz as Black people,
we are very *special*.

most of us dont know how
to be slaves and be cool.
so they build these special pens
for all those who wld be giants
and becuz a smart niggah
is a thorn in a dumb crackas side,
special places are designated
to contain their resistance.
special procedures are designated
to pry their souls away from their bodies
so they can be categorized as animals

cuz they aint got no souls!

like i sd.

they dont always wanna kill u
they just wanna make sure
that (if u're a man)
u aint out there on the streets
helpin Black youngsters to be men.
yeah, they wanna be sure
u aint out there bein real to some sistah
protecting her mind
body and soul from the freaks
who come alive and thrive at the slightest mention
of a male shortage.

they dont always wanna kill u.
they just wanna stall yr development
long enuff for u to forget that u're a man.
and they figure if they catch'chu early enuff
they can snuff out yr spirit sooner
cuz lawd knows
aint nothin more troublesome
than a niggah who thinx he's a man.

whether u can dig it or not
we are all inmates of the same asylum.

we cannot teach our children who they are
w/out riskin our lives;
we cant move to keep ourselves secure
w/out bringin the sky down on us
i.e. police, state troopers,
nat'l guard, marines, etc.

our prison:

is so cozy, so comfortable,
we really dont mind livin here
as long as we can get color'd
in & on t.v.
cuz basically,

we think we're in hollywood
starrin in action-packed movies
& there's plenty of excitement, cuz it's a fact
that niggahs get chased more
than any otha people in the world ! ! !

most people figure that prison
is just something we have to live with,
like wite people,
but most people change their minds,
when it's their relatives bein hauled away
goose-stepped in the head,
nightstick'ed in the groin
by beings who w/out their uniforms and guns cldnt
equal a rat's turd.

and like i sd.

they dont always wanna kill u.
they wanna de-brace u
make u feel lower than the lowest form of life.
they wanna humiliate u
until yr interest in tomorrow is completely cancelled!
they dont always have to kill u.
sometimes they just bug u to death
by tellin u shit like yr old squeeze
is squeezin on somebody new
& what can u do

not knowing fact from fiction.

this is how they torture u by walkin on yr face
& leavin footprints on yr eyes.

and

whether u can dig it or not,
we are all inmates of the same society.

we cannot do anything we want
anytime we want to.

cuz throughout our midst
somebody's always ready to snitch.

and whether u believe it or not
most folks are in jail becuz they are Black.
becuz they are the descendants of more than
slaves & to this day are not allowed to live
with any kind of self-determination!

most folks are in jail
becuz they are needed as a cheap labor force
to do work that even aliens wld not do
most folks once released will return to jail
becuz this society
won't teach them how to survive
in a technological future.

a society that everyday
invites them to kill each otha
becuz the real enemy
is obviously untouchable.

most people are in prison
becuz they are not lucky like u & i.
& the only reason we are not in prison
is cuz our numbers didnt come up.
but rest assured the game of genocide
has many, many faces.
and those of us who arent physically locked up

are mentally fucked-up!

meanwhile:

back on the plantation,
the g&e goes up,
the c&p goes up,
the food goes up
and housing gets scarce
taxes go up
and ways to pay them disappear
becuz jobs are unavailable

and programs of assistance are few
and health goes down
but medical costs rise and scrape the sky.

and people be actin crazi
but that's how u spozed to act
when somebody be tryin to squeeze u
off the earth.
and as new & improved prisons go up
(not to alleviate over-crowdedness but to make room for
the new victims soon to be locked up)

more people go down!
just becuz they wanna live
by any and all means possible.

so dig it!

next time u hear a siren, dont go lookin around

to see who it's comin for *assume*
it's comin for u

      & do what'chu gotta do!

beno's song #1

how hard is the stone
where u stay locked away
from the tenderness
i am storing in yr namesake/to later build a monument
in honor of yr quiet,
Black strength.
how loud is the silence
where yr ears can never fully escape
the assault of otha's grunts and midnite groans.
how monotonous are the soundz
of othas, stirring about in the misery
of their own bits/a bit/yeah.
that's what they put in horses' mouths
when they be tryin to break'em.

only this time,
they've caught an unusual breed of stallion
a lover of Blackness.
tho momentarily corral'd
one day u will again chase the wind.
and again, the earth will tremble
when u run.

we are the chosen ones
aint nothin mystical bout that;
we have chosen ourselves
to be guardians for our people. and together we are a
most fierce phenomena: becuz the way we can sometimes
vibe on each otha /in the middle of all this primitive shit,
is the only evidence of hope for this world.
(this is not a pome. . . this is a fact).

my ole man

(for Arizander Robinson)

my ole man was never old.
he was only 15 yrs older than me.
yet the ways of all men jazzed behind his eyes.

i cld sing for him
but i'm a woman now
and my song wld probably sound like the whinings
of all the otha women
who wanted to be a part of him.

to his face i usta question his wild ways
and he wld question my questions,
fearing and knowing
that i was the embodiment of his spirit
looking him right dead in the eye.
how difficult it must have been for him
to see himself more in his daughter
than in all of his sons.

when i was young,
i wld go diggin into the nite to find him.
needing his presence for balance,
and his smile for reassurance.
otha men were offered to me as surrogate daddies
but as long as he was alive, who needed them?
and besides,
i was a thick-rooted child
and no one's seed but my father's
cld claim me as fruit.

the man i knew as father
caused me to go wandering out
into the shadows lookin for men just like him
—to treat me like he treated women.
wite men kidnapped him,

and caged him so many times
that his gaping absences left me with holes
in my woman-thing.
holes that i'm still tryin to fill with pomes, musik,
and men who promise not to hurt me
too much.

as wite people destroyed the means
for Black alternative livelihoods to survive,
my father shrank into himself
all his hurts and all his "ifs"
were violently jammed into his soul
where no one was allowed to go:
not prying women lookin for an edge,
or needy children lookin for guidance.

the man i dubbed father
wanted to kno what it was i was always tryin to get out
of him. . .
why was I so persistent about dialogue. . .

why i wldnt just go away when dismissed. . .
why i was always testin him for tenderness. . .
why i wldnt just stop needin his luv so much
and go on about my estrogenic bizness.
but i just kept resurfacing, saying
"i'm yr daughter,
and u belong to me."

he knew that,
but i reminded him anyway.
and when circumstances finally slowed his roll
to an imperceptible crawl
and he was forced to live at his motha's house,
i luv'd knowing that the dayze
of going to bars, and pool-halls,
and sad, fast women to leave messages for him
were gone.
that now i cld find him,
even if i wanted nothin greater than a hug.

once i knew he was centralized,
i demanded that he extend himself to me.
becuz i had spent most of my life
tryin to protect and defend the precious reality
of our being father and daughter
and i felt we were finally in a position
where i cld get some of that energy back.

the man i called father
once lived in hell
w/out being reduced to ashes
he walked on two legs
when only crawlin was allowed
and for this,
a greater man can hardly exist for me
for whether positive or negative,
he was always a man of power
and as flesh of his flesh
i will always be the radiance
generated by that power.

mema

(for my grandmotha)

from u i extract the sap
of heroines gone by.
my spirit flexes enuff muscle
to smite a thousand bloodless enemies.

from u i catch spectrums of
ancient light.
beams of race-memory
fire from yr hair &
grabbing them outa the air
i turn them into poetree
with which to heal the spirit
& raise the dead to their esteemed heights.

u are the prayer that un-locks
the temple that shields my soul
where the ancestors assemble
to weave on their terrible looms.

u are the beginning, middle & the end
of all the many-splendored things
that i've ever aspired to be.

sistahs cant be bros in my book

i luv Blackmen.

i luv Black women.

and, i luv the sameness of them
almost as much as i luv the differences.

i luv the way my softness
grafts onto a man's firmness.
luv the way they try
to drape logic all over an emotional situation.

i luv the way
they are protective of me
even when i dont necessarily need it.

soooooo,

when one of my Black and beautiful sistahs
tries to press her breasts against mine
hoping to trick my body into believing
promises hers cant keep. . . i get mad.

cuz her preference is her bizness,
but she does not have the right
to impose it upon me
under the guise of sisterhood.

if i put my arms around her, it's becuz i care about her
not becuz i wanna get it on.

& if that's what she thinx
then she has mistaken my sisterness
for something only *menandwomen* can claim.

and she has no right
to push her pelvis up against mine
in gross imitation of the kind of men
i've always hated, anyway.

where the bitchery ends,
sisterhood begins

dont roll yr eyes at me
u dont even kno me
and if something evil were to jump off right now,
i might be the only person willing to help u.

don't stand in the corner
whispering about me
if u wanna kno something about me /ask me!
the fact that i dont work my thing
the way u do doesnt mean u have the right
to hold me in contempt.

my name is not bitch,
tramp
or slut
and if u dont want yr man
to communicate with me then keep him home,
but dont get mad with me
for being polite enuff to dialogue with him
even though i'm not one of yr chosen few.

just becuz u & i dont gel
doesnt mean u shld turn yr kitty-kat friends
against me too.
how can my anguish
possibly make u feel good?

u & i arent strangers.
we ustah rule the world together.
we fought & escaped slavery together.
we cut each otha's cords
& gave birth together.
we cut the ropes
& buried the lynched together.
we've rescued each otha from crazi men

& licked our wounds together.
we've rejoiced in the coming of men
& wept at their departures;
and no matter how grossed-out life appeared
we handled it *together.*

so why are u acting like u dont kno me?

why are u lookin at me
out of the corner of yr eyes
tryin not to see my pain,
my situation,
my oppression.
why are u tryin to act like yr life is alright
but i'm the one with the problems?

why are u actin
like u've got more in common with miss anne,
than me?

why are u tryin to deny that part of u
that is also me?
think about it.

when men are not involved
we are seldom at odds.

think about it.

we blossom from the same stems
and treat each otha like poison ivy
instead of afrikan violets.

think about it.

the core of all our afflictions
is witer than the blood
that is Black like we.
returning to the source
doesnt mean u have to wear yr hair like mine,
or dress like me or think and act like me.
why waste time

on our differences when we cld be basking
in the similarities.

from the beginning of any time that mattered,
we have worked our hips thru-out history
conceiving civilization after civilization
while givin the Blackman
something voluptuous to hold.
we have moaned on our thrones,
sang in huts,
cried in chains,
laughed in the fields
& screamed in technicolor
the ultimate tale of our luv for our men.

and as we now face
an overwhelmingly brutal hour
let us use our beulah-mae-nzinga powers
to celebrate our luv for one anotha.

let this be the day we burn bitchery
& invoke sisterhood from its ashes.

let's start embracing each otha
& mean it.
let's ask sincerely about each otha
& mean it.
let's listen to each otha
& mean it.
let's comfort each otha
& mean it.
let's respect each otha
& mean it.

let's join our kings
& queen it!

fifty sleep-overs later

marry me?   huh!
he say he leavin, to find hisself a sistah
who wont ask for so much
and the news i got for him is
sooner or later
        we *all* do.

contraceptus interruptus

when i asked him
what kind of birth-control he used.
he looked at me
like i was crazy.
and the flesh he wanted to mesh
was three times hard and soft again
before he finally realized
he wasnt gettin in.

so u found out he slept with somebody else

and, i'm sorry.

but her name is not bitch, slut, or ho.
sometimes, the otha woman
is just anotha woman
who wants what u want. . .

so u found out u're not the only one,

                    and, i'm sorry.

but at least u kno about her
how do u think she's gonna feel when she finds out about
u,

                the otha woman.

and it doesnt matter what happens next
cuz in the end u'll still be sistahs
who tried to sip happiness
from the same fountain
and almost went to war til u realized,
it was the water that was no good!

just becuz u believe in abortion doesnt mean u're not pro-life

(for Dr. Gunn)

recently i read a medical report
that claimed women who had abortions
were not traumatized.
the person who said that, shld have been aborted.

it was probably some right-to-lifer
who believes that all pregnant women
shld be made to have babies
even if they've been raped,
even if it was incest,
even if it means their sanity,
even if they cant take care of a baby.

that same right-to-lifer
wants children to have the right to be born
in dire poverty,
to have the right to live with rats and roaches
to have the right to have a number instead of a name,
to have the right to be born
into a situation they cant possibly live thru.

just let the babies come;
it doesnt matter what they're coming into;
it doesnt matter whether they're wanted or not;
it doesnt matter whether they'll be welcomed
by crack-heads,
alcoholics,
pimps or molesters.
cuz lifers believe in quantity not quality,
and they almost never volunteer
to take care of some of these babies
they want to force to be born.
yet, when it comes to killin babies

in somalia, uganda or yugoslavia:
no problem.
no demonstrations.
no blocking the entrance of invading armies.
no protests against dropped bombs.
they only understand the concept of life
within the context of amerika,
which everybody knows is the center of dead meat.

to hear the lifers tell it,
it's a pleasure for a woman to lie up on a table
and have her insides sucked out
by a human-eater-vacuum-cleaner.
they think all u have to do is blink yr eyes
and u're thru
and ready to go to the club later, to meet mr. destiny.
yet some lifers are women
who wear make-up
which they're too stupid to kno
was made from the dead fetuses.

lifers wanna tell u it's murder to abort a fetus.
and i say, if it must be done,
it's better to abort at 3 weeks
than at 13 yrs of age.
look at our city streets
and watch the unwanted children
walkin, beggin, sellin, rippin, killin:
becuz nobody wanted them,
and they kno it.

lifers claim they've got the church on their side
(hell, the church started chattel slavery) and let's not
talk about the bones
that have so often been found
when convents were torn down.
they say the wrath of God
will visit anyone
who has an abortion.

but i got news for them:
most women punish themselves more severely
than God ever cld or wld.
and any God that cant forgive,
needs to be replaced.

nobody really wants to get up on that table.
nobody really wants to kill a part of themselves.
nobody wants to meet their ancestors with blood on their
hands but when a woman knows
she *cant* handle bringing a new life into fullness
she has *more than* the right,
to beg that life's forgiveness,
and send it back to the spirit world.

there are women who say
they dont believe in abortions
and they have baby after baby
by man after man
and their children suckle themselves on empty tits
and later kill somebody over a pair of tennis.
there are men who say
they dont believe in abortions
and they knock the women up at night
and say good-bye in the morning.
and like bees
they go from flower to flower,
flying forever away from tiny faces
that look just like them.

i hate this society
for creating an atmosphere so terrible
that good, clean women
feel compelled to stop life
from crossing the mightiest threshold
and yet i thank the Mother-God for the technology
that allows a woman to free herself
from the possibility of becoming a horrible mother.

and before i be a slave

even though it came w/out invitation
the movement inside her was still her only
definition of joy.
but there was to be nothing Afrikan
about this birth.

no proud father,
no helping sisters,
no celebrating clan.
just a foreign land where she squatted
in a screamless altered state
til a bloody, squealing thing
fell from her to the ground.

and the faces of all her ancient mothers
appeared in the baby girl's one.

and she kissed her and squeezed her.
baptized her with consecrated tears.
yes,

she adored her
and loved her
while crushing her enslaved head
with a liberating rock
that sent her soul winging back
to the spirit world
where blood-hounds cld never chase her
and no wite man cld rape her.

freedom's divas should always be luv'd

(for H. Tubman & Dr. Welsing)

i like to think
that somewhere between the bodacious flights
and unbelievable weariness
a quilted cloud was laid out on the ground
and a big, sudanese-looking war-lord
dropped his weapons and a fragile creature
of living ebony fell into his arms laughing
as she imagined the look on ole marse tom's face
when he realized his ten best field niggahs were gone.

i like to think,
that history just never got his name,
but that when harriet came in from off the road
(underground, that is)
there was food on the table,
a fire in the hearth,
and the general understanding
that he wld reverse her aches
and turn them into derringers
that she cld stuff in her clothes
for protection on her next trip.

becuz freedom was & shld always be the goal
of every Black person on the planet

i like to think
that when harriet was gearing up
for her next rescue mission
that he argued to go with her,
to help her, to hold her if
a sleeping fit came.
to protect her from possible capture or betrayal.
i like to think

that in the end she always left
with as much of him as he cld part with
and still stay alive.
that he gave his blessings and did spiritual
somersaults
to gain God's attention
to make secure harriet's tenacious back.
i like to think that he left every pore open
to try and gauge
even from a distance.
if harriet was alright.
that sleep rejected his advances
as long as absence left her side of the bed empty
and his nuller than void.

i already know that her love of God
and race were impetus enuff to send her out
into the ignominious night
to emancipate her people
from the festering bowels of slavery.
this i know w/out a doubt!
and i like to think that
he licked her wounds, and washed her hair,
and placed wild-flowers on the table before her,
and picked her up to put her to bed
and made her infinitely know
that she was the only one.

                    and when she stayed away
                    one night longer than estimated,
              i like to think
              he cried
          not wanting to live,
      if she died.

becuz i love harriet,
i had to speculate this pome.
becuz i love harriet, and
i've been planning

some midnight raids of my own.
becuz i love harriet
for showing me how to actively love Black people,
until i agreed to
letting that one principle rule my life.
i love harriet
for pointing me towards freedom
& making me fight for it myself.

i adore harriet and when it comes
to being loved by a Blackman
i like to think she had it like that
and if she didnt
        she shldve!

a natural kind of abolitionist

too young to ravish
she was a bellywarmer

functioning in a way,
that wld even make a dog revolt.

her vagina was a hotel under construction,
promising luxurious accommodations at a later date.

til then
she was a bellywarmer.
or something wite men used to rest
their feet upon til rape became more feasible or
rewarding, whichever.

& having been suckled by a momma
whose tribe swallowed swords,
she grew spikes out of her belly.
& when the wretched finally crawled up on her
seeking entrance into her holy-of-holies
she impaled them with warrior-queen strokes.
now, just how many of them she took out
is not as important as the fact that
every time paleness pushed her thighs apart,
she sent anotha generation

straight to hell.

just say no

(for Loogie)

when yr friendly gyn tells u
u'll have to have a hysterwrecktomy
just say no. if it aint life and death,
just say no.

when yr good ole doctor
tells u one will have to come off
just say no. if it aint life or death,
just say no.

       this carving out the insides of women
           as if they were pumpkins
              has got to stop.

       this padding of insurance reports
           at the expense of women's
              most precious parts
     is like a bounty
         that men pay other men
            if they can turn in
               enuff wombs and
                  breasts at the end
                    of the day.
    western medicine rivals hitler
       in murder & mayhem.

so if they tell u/u've got to be cut
take it to the Mother-God
she'll understand.
there's more in this world to healing
than what glistens sharply in
the hands of man.

dont be afraid to try wholistic medicine.
dont be afraid to change yr diet.
dont be afraid to try homeopathic cures.

dont be afraid to try acupuncture.
dont be afraid to fast & pray.
be afraid of anybody who wants to cut u
tune yr entire being up to say

hell no!

thru GOD there must be a better way!

restoring the queen

yr mouth is a cavern hiding spring
which my tongue discovers and shares
with my frazzled sensibilities.
the honey-ginger baby of my latest dreams,
u spice me
into forgetting the bland heroes
who pilfered my inner-cabinets
not becuz they were thieves
but becuz they were hungry.

and just when i thought bareness was my destiny,
here u come
replenishing my juices faster than i can absorb.
and oh,
the way u tend my fires
making my locks stand on the top of my head
in a salute to love and the ecstasy
of being allowed to be my illustrious self.

cant turn a famine into a feast

she really didnt want to sleep with anyone but him.
but when it came to sex
he seemed to dish himself out sparingly,
as if some exotic delicacy.
she really didnt want to melt with anyone but him.
but when it came to sex /the same match
never seemed to lite both their fires.
she was a long-distance runner and
he was a champion sprinter.

and she was really trying to be monogamous.
trying to show by her behavior
that she understood the implications of AIDS.
trying to show with pressed knees,
that he was the only one.

but he only came around once in a blu moon
didnt seem to need the therapy of her thighs.
didnt really seem to need
to include her in his real life.

she really didnt want to sleep with anyone but him.
but she was so hungry for something substantial.
so starving for gratification in its ultimate sweetness,
and someone young was coming to town
to seek anotha lesson/blessing.
some young one was coming back to town
to test himself for excruciating sensitivity
and the swollen flesh'd ability
to just burrow a path straight thru to joy.

she told her self to abstain, as a gesture of sincerity
a show of strength & really love.
but she was so hungry for the tlc
she had experienced in otha lives
and he had no intentions
of being a feast, now that he knew

he could be a famine &
still get whatever he wanted.

and the sweet young thing came in the midnight hour
stripped her libido of abstinence
destroyed her hunger
and drove her make-shift monogamy
back into the fairytale from whence it came.

i cld organize my blessings

i cld organize my blessings around u
designate moments out of every one of my days
for the rest of my life
to do something that will brighten
all the stars in yr world.

i cld establish a love-filled compensation fund
for u alone to draw from
whenever u need freedom from a memory
that threatens to wipe u out
with a pain that u never ever shlda had to endure
in the first place.

i cld get our ancestors
to tie-a-dye of love over us
spell us into a heavy need of one anotha
a mega-mutual desire
to mold, carve and paint the world
into something we can proudly
and surely hand-over to our children
as a sweet act of duty.

in ways that i cant be with othas,
i cld be with u alone
for long periods of sandy-beached time.
in ways that for a long time u wont be able to believe
i, as a healing herb
will be the greatest preventative of heartache
u will ever kno.

oh yeah.
i cld organize my blessings around u big time
but the question is
cld u stand such organization
or the magnitude of the blessings?

while hanging on to the edge of yr eyes blinking

(for E.B.N.)

let's not talk of luv. what good wld it do?
it's more than enuff to say,
that i like u too much.
every shadow that falls over yr face
becomes a being whose butt i kick
until yr smile returns.

so, let's not talk of luv. let's play it safe.
and peruse this day away under the covers.
let's read each otha in silence and avoid saying
anything that may be usable later.

let's be acrobats of some lost art of the heart
and very skillfully blow each otha's minds.

                    u are not mine to have

so let's not talk of luv.
aint it enuff that i'm keyed into yr every move
that i hang on *to the edge of yr eyes* blinking.
and recently, my days qualify themselves
according to how much i give of myself to u.

so let's understand that luvs not an issue here.
it is enuff that i've been secretly clocking my existence
to the rhythm of yr pulse/ happy or sad.
the door of my inner-sanctuary is open
take what u need from me.

after midnight

after midnight
the autumn tinted fibers of yr masculinity
have spider-webbed me into a carnal shelter
that i plead never to leave.

and in the dark enclosure, that is
yr adoration wrapped therapeutically
about my needing limbs/ i pulsate
in aching response to yr masterful fingering.

zambezi blood rushes where u touch . . .
and the earth of me *quakes*
as u continue to dive
and dive . . .

nearing the holy site
where my soul stands ready
to receive yr magnificent spirit
now/and a thousand pleasures after!

night-crawlers

if u're beautiful
and someone tells u so
it's only natural that u believe them.
some of us hear this kinda thing all the time
but, when people treat us
as if we're commodities
existing solely for their consumption
   sooner or later
we havta put on a bitch uniform,
just to get some respect!
but they tell us we're beautiful
so they can get something they think we have
something they must possess
or else lose their membership
in the dick-of-the-month club.
and after they get it
after they leave us breathless and believing
and looking
forward to the next time
their libidos threaten to self-destruct
and the only way their lives can be saved
is between a brand new pair
of "beautiful" thighs.

burnt skin dont scratch off like toast

i can't hurt u
like u hurt me,
becuz i am not a man living in a man's world.
and there are no strings within u
sensitive enuff to be plucked into a song
like the one u made me sing.

some people say i sound bitter,
and one day, i might.
but right now,
i sound like somebody who's been used up
and thrown away,
but most animals, when wounded,
are not too selective about how they scream.
consider me baby seal,
bludgeoned almost to death
and weigh my grief against bitterness.

in a manner most felonius

with diseased intent,
some niggah stole my wallet
violated my existence.

some niggah (to whom honor is unknown)
slithered along the ground,
raising himself only,
to open my storage bin
and steal my stuff.

every piece of paper that says who i am
was in that purse, let alone,
the only money i had in the whole world.

some low-life staked me out
spied on me,
and then pilfered my space
like some ominous, crawling thing
that (in the movies)
whole towns come out to kill
to save the community.

and if justice be a blind woman
i hope she seduces him into a coma
and surgically removes
whatever part he used to steal my shit.

the eviction

they touched my underwear.
handled my diary,
destroyed my altars without missing a beat.

with destructive precision,
they ripped my pictures from the walls
bagged my books as if they were so much trash.
bent my records, stole my camera,
gun and watch. and before the week-end came, they got
paid.
for trashing a Black woman's apartment,
they got paid.
for breaking my peace,
and violating my privacy—they got paid.
may the God of retribution pay them for real.

mass media mania

while wite people are quietly
and sneakily uniting forces around the globe
to do battle with their eternal enemies
we are waiting for kriss-kross
to wake up to the double-cross
that induced them to mis-lead
& mis-represent Black youths.

while wite people are closing Black schools
and sabotaging Black colleges
we are goin to the hair-dressers
instead of tryin to put something in our heads.
while wite people take bread out of our mouths
to feed russian people
who a couple of years ago
were amerika's worst adversaries
we are fast-fooding ourselves into cretinism
and wondering why we dont feel good.

while wite people are surgically
expanding their penises
we are waiting for tlc to identify
what it is they are clutching
when they grab themselves between the legs.

while wite people are fighting gun control
and arming themselves
with every conceivable weapon
we are arming our heads with new handkerchiefs
and cruisin for a gangsta bitch.

and while wite people are giving melanin people
hiv+ thru immunization programs
Black women are thrusting their g-strapped pelvises
into every camera that video will allow.

while wite people are fightin
over whether or not homosexuals
shld join the military
shanaynay is tryin to decide whether or not
to get a sex change
so she can impersonate martin lawrence
impersonating a real Blackman.

while wite people are reaching out
to their distant, foreign cousins to share oscar awards
Black people are singin, dancin & sittin on the edge
of their seats waitin for their names
to be called into glory
by people who not only wont honor them,
but wish they had died in their momma's wombs.

while wite people wait graciously
for the filmmakers to capture the grand stand-off in
waco, tx
Black people are gettin drunk
off of livin color in an effort to forget
that several years ago,
it was philly instead of waco;
the people were Black instead of wite;
and the results were dead children
lying in their own blood, and the destruction
of 60 homes:
                not a miniseries.

and while wite people convince the world
not to believe their lying eyes
and prepare to vindicate the 4 devils
who beat up rodney king
Black people are takin it all in with a grain of salt
as they add new items to their reparations list.

while wite people play pin-the-tail on the donkey
with clarence thomas & mike tyson
Black people scream racism

but when the issue was tawana brawley
there were only whispers.

and while wite people move forth
to cancel out their greatest fear,
while they build bigger prisons
to confine the objects of their fear,
while they mix up stronger forms of crack,
beat more Blackmen to death,
allow more Black children
to be adopted by wite homosexuals,
and create more melanin-centered diseases

Black people are rappin more and sayin less;
workin on cruder videos and less phd's;
raising fewer children
and having more babies;
laughin at the debasement of otha Black people
and crying more about being dis-respected.

wite people are putting their differences aside
to deal with us and we are arguing
about the mythical problems
of Black male-female relationships;
worrying about who will win the play-offs,
and goin to funerals
where the coffins are growing
smaller and smaller.
given the technology of the times,
wite people are planning
to rape the world again
while Black people are trying to decide
whether to write their own destiny
or let wite people write it
and wait for the movie.

let us pray

(to the Rodney King beaters)

adulthood
in the context of afrikan consciousness usa
is an accelerated state of dynamic being
changes change us into
that which has no adjectives.
while the future of even anotha moment
threatens us with gloomy visions
greater than the ones we've already had
and swore cld not be surpassed.
and somewhere between the hiv
and the crackhouses,
between the single sistahs
and the incarcerated brothas,
between the golf war and the presidential veto
of the civil rights bill, we re-define ourselves
while the horrors of living with wite supremacy
make us re-define the boundaries
and benefits of prayer.

a God is the spiritual embodiment
of the people who pray to it.
only Black Gods listen to Black people.
so to my Afrikan God of Divine Holiness,
please hear me when i say *yes*,
i hate'em and i want each one of them to die
a klan-induced Blackman's death
on a remote dirt road
in Killaniggah, Mississippi,
on the night of Malcolm X's next birthday.

amen. amen. amen.

steppin off on the x-wearers

(for Kwashi & Olu)

for u there will be no audubon ballroom,
only the dehydrated cries of yr people
as they lower u into the ground of absurdity
where yr confused souls hover
too bazaar, beserk & bewildered
to even reincarnate.

wearing malcolm's image
u move like a rat seekin a hole.
u blatantly sell drugs, eat pork, make babies
disrespect elders, put each otha down,
cut each otha up
and blow each otha away
while hiding behind the malcolm
that u claim is yr hero.

but what u luv is malcolm's lower-self
that self he murdered
for holding his manhood hostage.
u luv malcolm the hustler and pimp,
not the malcolm who transformed himself,
metamorphosized his people
and forced wite people
to respect and reassess their enemy.

u tell yrselves that u too are soldiers
when u dont even kno what side u're fightin on.
u luv the fact that malcolm's lower-self
once had him under control
and u use that fact to excuse yrself
as u knowingly sell madness and death
to yr people, with an X on yr chest
u speed along the streets
blasting counterintelligence musik

instead of being in school;
wearing an X-cap
u stand in front of somebody else's property
callin young sistahs bitches and ho's;
in yr X-sweatsuits with the pants hangin off the edge
of yr indiscreet behinds
u whip out 9mms and compete with police
in who can kill the most Blackmen
in the least amount of time.

u cld deal with big-red
but even malcolm X's toe-nails
were too heavy for u to comprehend.
u cld identify with malcolm's earlier responses to racism,
even copy them
but u cant and wont deal with the fact
that he came back from the grave.
he didnt stay there whining and crying
about wite people.
he burst back into the living.
instead of self-destructing
& forcing othas to do the same,
he escaped eternal membership with the living dead
instead of surrendering his balls to the killers of afrikan
people.

u dont luv malcolm.
u just use his face to make othas think u're down.
u dont luv malcolm.
u just use his past to justify yr fear
of facing yr real enemy
and yr inability to control yr own bowels.
the malcolm u luv
was the duckling, not the swan.
becuz luving malcolm the swan
means changing every aspect of yr pitiful little lives
into stories yr children can tell w/out shame.

for the so-called luv of malcolm
we've got X-medallions, X-earrings,
X-caps, X-jackets,
X- sweatsuits, X-watches,
X-tee shirts, X-air fresheners,
X-coffee mugs, X-lunchboxes,
X-clocks, X-totebags,
X-rings, and no X-cuse
for why betty doesnt get a cent.

wearing malcolm's image shld be a privilege earned,
an honor bestowed upon those
who've proven themselves to be uncompromising
in the pursuit of the liberation of our people.

only the clean & the just shld be able to wear malcolm
the productive & the focus'd
the spiritual & the prolific
the maintainers & the detonators.
only the best & the blessed
shld be allowed to sport malcolm's image
no matter how many means be possible.

and as long as jeffrey dahmer
can take a deep breath and the four cops in la
can plan a future
maybe none of us shld wear a malcolm x anything,
anyway.

suckling the enemy

knowing thru every square inch of yr skin
that he defiled yr grandmotha's grandmotha,
how now can u lay
legs entwined with the demon?

from the coffers of our very souls
he has stolen us from ourselves
in addition to our resources,
labor and genius,
u now offer him our melanin
as if it were something
u cld cop some more of downtown.

wite men are systematically killin Blackmen
at a mind-blowin rate
& u are givin them blow-jobs
in between the killings.

how do u think brothers feel
when wite men stomp on their genitals
while u slip into something a little more comfortable
& a lot less conscious.

how do u think i feel
when i see those swine lappin up yr pearls
while the rest of us try
to hold up the race without yr help, love or concern?

our identities are welded together
in blood, history & circumstance.
u cant have him as yr lover
and me for yr sistah
as long as he runs a world
that specializes in the collecting
of castrated Black penises.

all yr reasons are out of season
when it comes to how u wound up with him.

if u operate in a world
where there's no room for Blackmen
then u don't belong there, either.
if, as u claim, u're living on a monetary level
that excludes brothas,
before u go offering everything u've got
to some poorly-pigmented predatory punk,
maybe u'd better take yrself
down to alabama somewhere
& getchu one of those home-grown,
corn bread fed Blackmen
who've been raised to luv one woman til they die.
it cldnt hurt to try.

our momentary lack of unity
does not mean that we
are not accountable to each otha
and somewhere down the line
u will have to stand
before the anguished souls of the lynched
& explain how u came
to sleep with the lyncher.

the dreadful dreads

decorating the beaches like
a rare and beautiful endangered species
locks reaching out for help
while wite girls suck blood from yr sexy veins.

never noticing for a moment, the loss of memory
u flick yr head back,
whiplashing hair into a gesture of being hot-shit
while yr genitals are barb-wired to some wite witch,
whose check-book makes u cum;
and whose baby blue eyes put u at ease,
and liberate u from the god-awful chore
of being a real Blackman!

moving thru the urban jungle,
u stride like a lion
immersed in the glory of yr simple self
as sistahs interview u with their senses
and wite girls flash the cash
that will pay for yr initiation
into that great society
of self-denying carnivores
who praise afrika by day
and mock the ancestors by night.

crowned with huge hunks of melanin-soaked hair
u give off an air of royalty
as u strutt into nubian functions
with lil orphan-annie by yr side
dressed in afrikan clothes.
as if u really thought yr sperm
cld afrikanize a cow's ear into being a silk purse.
as if u really thought
u cld dick-away her murderous ancestry;
as if u really thought

that our luv for u wld out-weigh
our memorable disdain for her.

the price of ignorance is often death
but there are those, like u,
who deserve special recognition
and so it shall be
that yr locks will be carefully wrapped around
yr balls as they remain forever on display
in the dumb-niggah section
of the colored museum
marked: dreadful dreads.

the night something precious was split open

(for Phil)

when his last hope
went up like the smoke
          from a medicine-man's blanket
he lost it.
i came running out of my apartment
just in time to see:

he was delirious. rabid.
excruciatingly out of touch.
he rolled around on the ground
like a man on fire.
from the darkest cave of his whipped emotions
truisms like hairy beasts
leaped from his mouth
and disappeared in the television night.
he was unbalanced:
sick, Black, and without status.
and he rolled around on the ground
like an animal in pain
cursing those closest
for seeing his nakedness.
instead of hugs and soothings,
he got 3 wite police and one Black police woman.
and instead of being seized upon by capable friends
and forced into the peacefulness of home,
his face was stared into by a wite face
that didnt give a fuck about him;
while all around confused brown eyes
tried to register what was going on.
there was the bleeding absence of fatherly love,
there was the diseased absence of brotherly love,
and in the last deranged moments

there were only women.
offended by his behavior.
only women,
like the way he was raised.
and it was only the women
who whisked him away.
another state later,
he is again with only women,
left to imitate, find, discover manhood
in a maleless vacuum
of mammary glands and ultimatums
to do the right thing.
shld we wish him luck?

frustration in the gyrations

in the corners, they danced
while the women sat pattin their feet,
hair tightnin with a frenzy.
so much the longing to be spun on the floor.
but the men rub-a-dubbed with shadows
while the women slowly mustered the courage
to dance alone on the open floor.

and the patterns of their lives
were rhythmically etched

in toxic isolation.

sanfran breakdown

out of vaginas they jump,
into anuses they plunge.
luv is somewhere in the corner
havin a nervous breakdown.
and even lust
is havin a hard time explainin
what's happenin here.

new yorked out

and the men were lookin at *themselves*.
didnt see the women passin by.
becuz they were lookin at each otha.
didnt see the women offerin
life and everything else of value.
cuz they were so enraptured with one anotha.
cldnt possibly see the women's lives
screamin by on their way to barren heights.
cldnt see the nation, demobilizing,
dissolving, dispersing.
cuz they only had eyes for each otha
and each otha was all they cld see.

to any brotha that fits

not tall or blond enuff
she luvs a niggah
who cant stand his own momma.

all that is africentric & good
she has offered him. but,
he'd rather eat shit on a golden tray
than give his vitals
to a dark-skinned woman.

and in response to his jungle fever,
i pray that emmett till
can share his neck marks
with him whose absence of race memory
qualifies him so much
to be lynched.

no cross-roads to even consider

what i can do for u, i will,
but stay out of my bed.

cuz that confuses me into believing that u care
for me, the way i care for u. and existing evidence proves,
that aint even true.

still i offer u the best possible friendship.
and my energies delight in being able to show u
live and direct, the true workings
of pan-afrikanism.
but stay out of my room, will u?
cuz that implies something special
and the breath that now connects us is ordinary
and used.

we do not snap, crackle and pop
at the thought of each otha. we do not
plan, wish or dream each otha up in intimate
future scenes. all we do is. . . my room.

and i'd rather we didnt.
however, u can still get from me
whatever i have it within me to give u.

but keep yr semen to yrself and leave my ovaries alone.
and maybe our expectations will mature and grow
into something worth nurturing.

who told u / u could put that on

1993 was the year of the bulge.

obesity thought it was in/called for the death of thin
while fatness went on a holiday.
from a land where mirrors are unknown
and all priorities are connected to eating
the spandex generation evolved
and e x p a n d e d
into a majority that needed to express itself
by cultivating eating into a perverse art.

they took to the streets like locusts.
stout. rotund. overloaded
like animated sausages
they wrapped themselves in fabrics that never covered
enough

in 1993, *modesty* committed suicide
and the fat girls told themselves they looked good
as they squeezed themselves into things that cld
not stretch.
they forced the world to look at them and
their cellulite, while they stuffed themselves
into knits and leather which clinged tighter to them
than to the cows from which they came.

somehow, somewhere,
they were brainwashed into believing they were *it*.
and they wobbled around, straining for breath,
while trying to put over some jive manifesto about fat
being attractive.
their common lack of discipline was twisted
into some new concept of fashion, which was tolerated
and whispered about by folks who knew that obesity was
a sickness
something u go get help for, instead of bigger and
brighter clothes.

the inability to push away from the table
is a leading cause of death among Black people.

there is nothing intelligent about not being able to carry
yr own weight w/out a cane.
if u cant run a mile in the inner-city,
u're askin for trouble.

if u cant look down and see the jewels of life shining then
you've committed a crime against yourself,
and all the life forms that grace yr sphere of influence.
though thin is not in, fat is not where it's at.

only moderation knows what's happening.
so come on take a look at yrself and moderate.

for a semi-precious moment

(for S.D.B. '89)

i only wanted to be with u for a
semi-precious moment.
i only wanted the best for u and yr well-being,
but u cut off my hands so i cldnt give,
ran off in yr car so that i cldnt follow.
i wldve agreed
to any arrangement u wanted
so long as it wld prevent separation.
but u sealed my mouth so i cldnt cry
for want of communication
and then u took me to a cliff
and when i wldnt jump, u pushed me off
with yr fear of commitment,
and u will be pleased to kno, that when last seen,
i was still falling.

u've got to pay

yeah, yeah, yeah
i luv too easily/ i know it.
a characteristic that has never been
to my credit. it seems to come natural to me
to appease a man's hunger
with a tincture of my own essence.

to the esoteric i am
a pure delight. but life to them
means something else.
never keeping me, only hangin on to me
for dear life.

to luv w/out logic is deadly.
to live w/out luv is absurd.

therefore, my expectations
have found their own voices.
no more luv for luv's sake.
i'm too old for maybe baby-isms.

the summer of me was stolen
by tall, Black bandits whose needs i just cldnt resist.
and before they overtake me on my new road,
lemme make something excruciatingly clear.
if u think u want even a taste of my luv
(i'm not talking money, here)
u've got to pay!
& no, i dont take lay-away.

a man like malcolm

i want a man like malcolm
to luv Black people with me
to be able to discuss carter woodson
under the covers with me.

i want a man like malcolm
to argue with
until i have to go back to the library
to make sure i kno what i'm talkin about.

i want a man like malcolm
so that when i feel a harriet tubman urge
i can go into action w/out having to worry
about whether the person i sleep with
has my back.

i want a man like malcolm to come home to
after i've had a hard day
of shakin the shit outa wite people.

i want a man like malcolm
to hold me the way he held us all,
tight against the chest
as if our existence revolved around him.

i want a man like malcolm
with a red-hot spirit to fire me up
into whatever form of steel my people need me to be.

i want a man like malcolm
to luv me with a fierceness
that can be used to coat my back-bone
with an indelible substance
that repels cowardice and selfishness.

i want a man like malcolm
to grow with me
into one incredibly sharp machete

that slices away at the the wite cancer
that consumes our race.

i want a man like malcolm
to help me create a child that in days of glory
i can look at and say,

u're just like yr father!

the yielding

i cup myself to offer yr lips the
quench yr soul's been thirsting for.
with hours of heart rendering,
and skin shedding rituals,
my loneliness has been exorcised
with seductive precision.
from deep within,
blue-Black passions culminate
and flashdance into a meteorite
prepared to shower u
with more sincerity than yr flesh
thinks bearable.
long-awaited tongues
thrust jasmine into the air.
spirits enter non-threatening dimensions
and exchange ecstacies.
polarities converge,
illuminating the atmosphere
with the prisms of
light that come pouring out of our Black guts
bursting in love,
to celebrate the death
of wite supremacy.

the ball is always in yr court

i kno u luv me.
u kno it too,
only u wont say the words
cuz u're afraid that
will somehow put u under my power
which shows u dont kno nothin bout power
cuz if i wanted to work somethin on u
the words wld come from me.

u kno i luv u,
by the way i open myself up to u
like a magical garden
which u are welcome to pass thru.
u kno i can live w/out u
which is why u wont commit yrself to me.
u dont want me to be able to live w/out u,
even though u wont live with me.
in a way it almost sounds like
u dont want me to live.
u want me to drown in yr image
while u sit on the dock, at the bay,
tryin to decide whether or not to be my life-boat.

u dont want me to have anybody else,
yet u only send yr ghost to be with me,
while the real u must keep pre-occupied
to keep from doin whatchu really wanna do
like be with me.
u always talkin bout how u got things to do
u aint got nothin to do but let me luv u,
if u only knew how.

yr way of luvin
has sent me back to the drawing-board
too many times,
just to find a way to convince u that i am not a threat.

there are no bombs inside me
waitin to explode when u touch me.

i'm not going to broadcast yr one-time inability
to get it up, in the news.
i am not going to hold a press conference
on yr flaws or yr fears.
and i cant use yr love to catapult me
into somewhere else,
cuz u are where i wanna be,
if u cld just see me
beyond the veil of testosterone
which cautions u to be cool.
just chill. dont let yr real feelings show.
make her want u.
and all the otha dumb stuff.

what i got for u
i cant give to anybody else.
and whether or not emotionally
u can put yrself in a receptive posture
can make all the difference between
whether or not u can evolve
into a world of unconditional loving and giving,
or whether u spend the rest of yr life
asking hungry women "is it good?"

    either way,

the ball, is in yr court, as usual.

half steppin thru history

when i first started studying our history
i wld read about slavery & say in conversation
"i cldnt have been a slave.
they'd have had to kill me."
and whoever i was talkin with wld readily agree.

yet here we are!

here we are
bound & gagged right here
in this sophisticatedly decadent,
blood-sucking center of the universe,
wearing $165 tennis-shoes
        marching for gay rights,
                and talkin bout what we wldnt have tolerated
believing even that had we been slaves,
we wld have been haughtier,
more insolent, meaner,
more oblivious to pain,
stone-cold in bearing the lash.
we think we wldve sucked our teeth,
thrown curses with our eyes,
& fought to the death rather than be sold!

bullshit.

we'd have made the same moves then that we do now.

wite people use behavior-altering drugs
on our male children so they'll be submissive in
school and even more submissive
when it comes to defending the race.

and we take it.

wite people bring drugs into our community
as if they were takin food to a starvin nation.

and we take it.

wite people test automatic weapons
by selling them to us to exterminate each otha.

and we take it.

they pay us the least & charge us the most
for everything & then
tax us when we buy something
& use the taxes to help everybody but us.

and we take it.

they kill us when they feel like it.
and they feel like it a lot.

and we take it.

so we shld just shut-up about slavery
& address the hell we're descending deeper into
right now.
& if we're not willing to die to liberate ourselves now
we wldnt have died
to escape slavery then, either.

we do our ancestors an un-fathomable injustice
when we claim that we wldve handled slavery
differently, better.

we suggest that they were
less than strong, somehow, not as defiant as we.
right now we cant even defy gravity
w/out ignorance holding onto our feet.

everytime one of our ancestors
lowered her or his head, and lived.
that same heart-swallowing gesture
turned into a rung on a ladder
that one of us climbed to reach the future.
their tears were the jewels we hocked
to help pay for our freedom.
and their whip marks were molded into the muscle
that we have yet to adequately use

to deliver ourselves from 20th century,
scientific bondage.

if we dont do the dynamic deeds
that will honor & vindicate our ancestors
. . .if we dont beat the devil back
into his frozen hell. . .our grandchildren's children
will be sitting around idly
talking about what they wldve done
had they been in our shoes.

if we dont snatch our souls from the jaws of the beast
no libations will be poured in our memory
our names will not be written in the halls of forever
and like the sahara
        the sands of time will bury us
                and claim we never existed.

domiabra

my heart was meant to be played by a virtuoso
meant to be massaged with high-low notes
of gut-wrenching joy.

if u're afraid to hear the soundz of luv
unhand me /and return me to the warmth of myself; for
my heart not to sing

is agonizing death for me.

livin in and out of the corners of each otha's eyes
we have danced this dance too long.
if u want a juju that will insure yr well-being
til the end of never's ever
if u want life's unsurpassed voltage
to breathe sweet lillies of wonder into yr every vein
if u want a warrior-queen to fight by yr side
til dust we both be

    domiabra: if u luv me, come.

what can i say to make u kno
yr presence on this planet is dangerously connected
to my lifesupport system.
i'm tired of days that do not include u.
without yr face to periodically grace
the lack-luster moments of my existence
—i languish

without yr eyes to lick me —i languish

without a clue from u on how deep
am i gettin to u baby —i languish.

the ruby-filled sands of my hour-glass
are passionately descending

    domiabra: if u luv me, come.

if u ever come under my blanket
be ready to forget the moments
u doubted my actuality.
be ready to forget the lucky nights
u spent in unfamiliar boudoirs.
if u ever wander into my hemisphere
be ready to forget the skins u took
in desperation /and kiss yr loneliness good-bye.

   domiabra: if u luv me, come.

* *in the Twi language of Ghana, Domiabra means: if you love me, come.*

the end of the revolution

if i stop right here, right now
i'll still have 23 yrs of struggle to my credit.
23 yrs of trying to do the right thing for us
even when it wasnt the right thing for me.
23 yrs of creating spaces for myself
in amerika, without a blue-print.
23 yrs of pushing blindly into this last frontier
with nothing to go on
but the sacramental voices of ancestors
who wont leave me alone.

if i stop right here right now
i'll still have given more than half
of my life towards our liberation.
half a life time of moving towards the light
even when darkness was tantalizing and
full of what i really needed.
half a life-time of denying myself a family
becuz the nationalistic puzzle pieces were not in place.
and my status in our liberation
demanded that i make more substantial choices
while silencing my own heart.

so what if i do stop
right here.
right now.
the r in revolution isnt locked in my being.
what do i care who bad-mouths me later on,
without walkin two steps in my shoes.
maybe the best i cld give, i've given,
and the rest is somehow meant for me.
so what if i do like the absence of under-wear.
and yeah, ive got a thing for leather.
so what if i wanna write my next book in bimini.
and who cares if i like men under 38.

and no, it doesnt take much
to make me dance, and yes,
that prince album in the corner belongs to me.
and this is where i'm at people
if i must struggle
then something sweet in struggle,
has got to be for me.

if u wanna kno how i feel about Blackmen just ask me

(for Imani)

the first man i ever knew was big, gruff
and the master of polygamy.
as my father's father/he laid claim to me
when i was only 6 mths old.
once i was nestled safely in his house
he let it be known to the world
that i was never going back to my motha's people. and
that was my first introduction to
afrikan-manhood.

my grandfatha saved my life and lost his own.
with his last wind he blew me
into the struggle /gave me his back-bone
and dared me to give it up!
the last twenty years have been a tornado of
events that tossed me around so passionately
that the only reality that i cld keep hold of
has been my luv for Blackmen.
so for all the doubters and simple-ass disbelievers
let's get the record straight once and for all.
the most consistent thing in my life has been my luv for
Blackmen.
and if i had a dollar for every heart-ache
i've suffered behind a bro
i cld buy amerika and give it back to the Indians.
and tomorrow, if my new luv throws me away
i'll come back into myself, take a break, clean off my
spirit, pray that i can understand & forgive, and then
move on to my new man.
and if that doesnt work out,

then i'll move on to the next one, becuz
i've got more than enuff luv to share. and even
though in yr anguish u wound me, mistreat me, or
abuse me, i'll never
let the behavior of some of u destroy my reverence for
all of u.

becuz i've seen what a Blackman can do
i'm hip to imhotep, and down with chaka zulu.

unless nat turner objected
i'd have been his personal body-guard.
if i'd been around in garvey's day
i'd have been competition for amy.
becuz i've had the pleasure of beholding the Blackman's
wonders,

i can testify to malcolm's manhood,
becuz it was so tight that air cldnt seep into it.
george jackson was so invincible
that the steel in his nerves was stronger
than the steel bars of his cell.
and marc essex showed us
that we neednt be terrified of wite people
becuz they too can be killed.
and then diop came along
with his multi-incredible self
to show us that discipline must be the key
to any lock we want to open.
and today we have dr. ben and dr. clarke
we've got haki, richard king, obenga and mandela.
with men like these, how can we lose?
and on a personal note,
i've got a publisher named paul
who worries more about my soul than my pomes
i've got imani, who worries about whether i have food,
i've got doc who worries about
whether or not my new luv is treatin me alright.

all these men belong to me.

they are my fathers and bros and lovers
and nothing anyone cld ever do cld make me stop
luving *Blackmen.*
becuz the Blackmen i've known are the ones who built
the pyramids
and they are actively changing and correcting
history with their every thought and action.

and i feel sorry for any sis who doesnt kno these men or
anyone like them.
becuz it's the few good ones that enable us to survive the
negative ones.
one straight-walkin, truth-talkin Blackman can absolve
the negativism of twenty Blackmen.

and no matter how many more painful experiences i
might have, no one Blackman will ever destroy my devotion
to all Blackmen.
no combination of Blackmen will ever make me turn my
back on all Blackmen.

so in the future
if anybody ever mentions my name to u
and asks u what u kno about me,
u can say straight from the heart
"i dont kno the sistah too well, but the one thing i kno
about her is she luvs herself some *Blackmen.*"

090718-200-5-60W